Bible Trivia
Quiz Book

Greg Cynaumon, Ph.D.

Additional books by Dr. Cynaumon can be
found by visiting www.dreamfocus.org

BARNES
&NOBLE
BOOKS
NEW YORK

The author wishes to thank Rick Campbell and Heather Russell-Revesz, as well as all the folks at Barnes & Noble Publishing for sharing the vision that a Bible trivia book presents a positive and fun way to learn more about the greatest book in history.

Finally . . . a debt of gratitude to my family—Jan, Tracy, and Matt for their love and support.

ISBN 0-7607-3068-7

Book design by Lundquist Design, New York

Printed and bound in the United States of America

02 03 MP 9 8 7 6 5 4 3 2 1

OPM

In the Beginning

Q: A famous mutiny, something you raise, and Adam and Eve's first son?

Q: True or false? Sarah and Abraham had the same father.

Q: Multiple choice: On what mountain did the ark come to rest after the Flood?
   (a) Olives   (b) Ararat
   (c) Horeb   (d) Vesuvius

Q: Jared was 962 years old when he died, but he was still not the oldest guy in the Bible. Who was the oldest and how old was he?

Q: What fugitive prophet slept in the bottom of a ship as it rolled in a storm?

A: Cain. (Gen. 4:1)

A: True. (Gen. 20:12)

A: (b) Ararat. (Gen. 8:4) It's easy to remember this place because when Noah checked rodents, two-by-two into the ark, he must have said, "Hey...you *ar-a-rat.*" (Sorry, couldn't resist.)

A: Talk about national debt! Methuselah could have collected approximately 902 years of social security before he died at age 969. (Gen. 5:20)

A: Jonah, as he was trying to hide from God, prior to volunteering to be tossed overboard to save the others. (Jon. 1:5)

Q: What do pork, shellfish, rabbit, and bats all have in common?
   (a) they're the "other white meat"
   (b) the Bible says not to eat them
   (c) they were considered sacred
   (d) they were considered a delicacy

Q: What prominent biblical figure actually sent his buddy off to war so he could "put the moves" on his friend's wife?

Q: There was once a young king mentioned in the Bible who pleased God greatly when he prayed for wisdom instead of wealth. Who was this king?

Q: Who sold their brother into slavery for 20 pieces of silver?
   (a) Judas   (b) Caesar
   (c) Joseph's brothers (d) Daniel's brothers

A: (b) We can't imagine why someone would have to be warned not to eat *bat*, but each of these animals is designated in scripture as "unclean" and therefore not kosher.

A: It was none other than good old King David who sent Uriah back to the war knowing he would be killed. With Uriah out of the way, David would be able to have Bathsheba for himself. Uriah met his maker and David committed a sin, but eventually saw the error of his ways, repented, and remained in God's favor. (2 Sam. 11:9)

A: Solomon. In fact, God told Solomon, "Since you have asked for wisdom and not for long life or wealth for yourself, nor have you asked for the death of your enemies, but for discernment in administering justice, I will do what you have asked. I will give you a wise and discerning heart, so that there will never have been anyone like you, nor will there ever be." (1 Kings 3:10–13)

A: (c) Joseph's brothers (the sons of Jacob) sold poor Joseph to the Ishmaelites for twenty lousy pieces of silver. Some estimate twenty pieces of silver to be equal to approximately $5.00 today. As you may recall, however, Joseph had the last laugh. (Gen. 37:28)

Q: What was the common unit of currency in the Old Testament?
(a) drachma   (b) shekel
(c) goats   (d) talents

Q: On which day of creation did God make the sun and moon?
(a) Thursday   (b) the first day
(c) the fourth day (d) the seventh day

Q: Which of the following characters were never named in the Book of Genesis?
(a) Joseph   (b) Moses
(c) Isaac   (d) Nimrod

Q: Besides being the only four beings in the Garden of Eden, what did God, Adam, Eve, and the serpent have in common?

A: (b) The shekel, which is still the unit of currency in Israel today.

A: (c) the fourth day. An interesting aside is that God created light on the second day—hence the phrase "Let there be light." So He had light on Day 2, but didn't bother with the sun or the moon until the fourth day. Technicalities!

A: (b) You, yourself may be a nimrod if you answered (d), because Moses himself doesn't enter scripture until the book of Exodus.

A: Lips notwithstanding, each could speak. In Genesis 3:4–6, the serpent talked Eve into eating from the forbidden tree of knowledge. The rest, as they say, is history.

Q: According to the Book of Genesis, why was the moon created?
   (a) to denote the passing of time
   (b) to light the night sky
   (c) for travellers to find their way
   (d) God was bored

Q: Who is the first person in the Bible to pray?
   (a) the serpent   (b) Adam
   (c) Eve   (d) God
   (e) Abraham

Q: There was one Old Testament food that the Israelites were allowed to gather only six days a week. What was the food?
   (a) lox and cream cheese   (b) matzo
   (c) manna   (d) fatted calves

Q: Unscramble this famous Bible quotation and name the book where it can be found:
   shall thy covet thou wife neighbor's not

A: (a) Much like a calendar, God created the moon to help mark the passing of seasons, days, and years. (Gen. 1:14)

A: (e) Abraham prayed to God to heal Abimelech, his wife, and his slave girls so they could have children again. (Gen. 20:17)

A: (c) They would gather manna (Exodus 16) in the wilderness. On the sixth day they were supposed to gather enough to see them through the seventh day when they would rest.

A: "Thou shall not covet thy neighbor's wife." (Exodus 20:17)

Q: Where did Moses live during his childhood?

Q: What is the name of the older brother of Moses?

Q: On what mountain did Moses receive the Ten Commandments?
(a) Mount Sinai   (b) Mount Olives
(c) Mount Carmel   (d) Mont Blanc

Q: Which of the following is not one of the Ten Commandments?
(a) Thou shalt not steal
(b) Thou shalt have no other gods before me
(c) Thou shalt not eat from the tree of knowledge
(d) Thou shalt not kill

A: In the court of the Pharaoh. Because the Pharaoh had ordered all male babies of the Israelites to be killed, Moses had been put in a basket beside the river, where the Pharaoh's daughter saved him. (Exod. 2:10)

A: Aaron. (Exod. 4:14)

A: Moses received the tablets on (a) Mount Sinai as found in Exodus 19. Mount Olives and Mount Carmel are closely associated in the New Testament, and Mount Blanc is an overpriced writing instrument.

A: (c), although God did forbid Adam and Eve to eat from the tree, it was not one of the commandments given to Moses on Mount Sinai.

Q: Who walked in the Garden of Eden in "the cool of the day"?

Q: According to the Old Testament, what kinds of people were rubbed down with salt?
(a) salty people   (b) babies
(c) the dead   (d) lepers

Q: Who bragged for forty days and taunted the Israelite army?
(a) Samson   (b) Goliath
(c) David   (d) God

Q: What type of wood did Moses use to build the ark?
(a) balsa   (b) cypress
(c) pine   (d) ash

Q: Who planted the first garden?
(a) Adam and Eve   (b) God
(c) It was never mentioned (d) Martha Stewart

A: God. (Gen. 3:8) Please tell us you didn't answer *the serpent!* You had a 33% chance of guessing right as only God, Adam, and Eve had legs.

A: (b) Tell us a little salt in your diaper wouldn't chap your behind! Apparently newborn babies were rubbed down with salt to purify them. (Ezek. 16:4)

A: (b) 1 Samuel 17:16. This is the story of Goliath, the Philistine soldier, who held the Israelite army off until David whacked him on the melon with a smooth stone out of his sling. A little known fact is that, contrary to folklore, Goliath did not stand thirty feet tall, but was more like seven to eight feet in height. Even at seven feet, Goliath towered over the average men in that day who were just above five feet tall.

A: Did you fall for it? This is a trick question because Moses did not build the ark! Try Noah, and by the way, he used cypress wood.

A: (b) God planted the first garden and then handed it over to Adam and Eve who were doing pretty well until the serpent (and not Martha Stewart) came along and messed things up. (Gen. 2:8)

Q: Who pleaded with God not to destroy Sodom
for the sake of forty righteous people?
  (a) Moses   (b) Abraham
  (c) the Sodomites   (d) Noah

Q: What two trees grew in the Garden of Eden
that don't grow anywhere else?
  (a) the tree of life and the tree of death
  (b) tree of life and the tree of wisdom
  (c) the tree of life and the tree of knowledge
  (d) fig and prune

Q: Why did God make the Israelites wander in the
wilderness for forty years?
  (a) to teach them to use a map
  (b) for their evil ways
  (c) they were not repentant
  (d) they mocked God

A: (b) Abraham did a wonderful job negotiating with God, but in the end, he couldn't save Sodom from self-destruction. The story of Genesis 18 and the conversation that takes place between God and Abraham features psychology at its best.

A: (c) Two trees stood in the middle of the Garden of Eden. They were the tree of life and the tree of knowledge of good and evil. As you know, the serpent manipulated Eve into eating the forbidden fruit from the tree of knowledge of good and evil by telling her that she could attain Godly wisdom. (Gen. 2:9)

A: (b) The Old Testament essentially explains their actions by saying that the Israelites had chosen to do "evil" and wandering through the wilderness for forty years was the price they had to pay. (Num. 32:13)

Q: What lump of dust came to life when God
   breathed into it?
   (a) the first dust bunny   (b) Adam
   (c) Eve   (d) the Serpent

Q: Noah had three sons. Two were named Japheth
   and Shem. What was the third son's name?
   (Hint: a holiday main course, someone who
   craves attention, and an amateur radio operator)

Q: In the beginning…who named the animals God
   created?

Q: Who was promised that their "eyes would be
   opened" if they disobeyed God?

Q: What did God place in the Garden of Eden
   because it was pleasing to the eye?
   (a) Eve   (b) trees
   (c) a lake   (d) shag carpeting

A: (b) History records what women have always
believed—"since the beginning of time, men are no
better than dust." The Book of Genesis records that
God used dust to create Adam, however, He designed
Eve to be more relational in nature and therefore
made her out of Adam's rib. (Gen. 2:7)

A: Ham. (Gen. 5:32) No points awarded for turkey, pork
chops, or Stove Top Stuffing®.

A: Most incorrectly believe God named the creatures in
the Garden of Eden. Actually, God delegated that
task to Adam. (Gen. 2:19)

A: Adam and Eve. This is one of the lies the serpent told
them to get them to eat from the tree of knowledge of
good and evil. (Gen. 3:5–7)

A: (b) Trees. Genesis 2:9 tells us that God planted every
tree because they were both pleasing to the sight and
good for food.

Bible IQ

Q: Many names of Bible characters appear strange in their original Hebrew or Greek. Take a look at the following list of names and try to guess his or her more familiar biblical name.

1) Yoseph
2) Timotheos
3) Aharon
4) Hevel
5) Shelomoh
6) Stephanos
7) Yehudhah
8) Markos
9) Miryam
10) Petros
11) Iesous
12) Adham
13) Andreas
14) Izevel
15) Kornelios

Q: God changed what man's name from one meaning "exalted father" to a name meaning "father of multitudes"? (Hint: Starts with "A.")

A: 1) Joseph
   2) Timothy
   3) Aaron
   4) Abel
   5) Solomon
   6) Steven
   7) Judah
   8) Mark
   9) Mary
   10) Peter
   11) Jesus
   12) Adam
   13) Andrew
   14) Jezebel
   15) Cornelius

A: Name changes are common throughout scripture. In this case, God changed Abram's name to Abraham, which meant "father of multitudes." (Gen. 17:5)

Q: Which prominent book of the Bible states that money is the root of all evil?

Q: Where was Paul when his compatriots prayed for daylight to come?
   (a) in the temple   (b) on a ship
   (c) at the movies   (d) in prison

Q: According to Paul, what should a person pray for when he speaks in tongues?
   (a) self-interpretation   (b) a tongue depressor
   (c) discernment   (d) silence

Q: According to the Book of Leviticus, what type of people had to walk around town shouting "Unclean!....Unclean!"
   (a) lawyers   (b) lepers
   (c) harlots   (d) adulterers

A: Actually this is a common mistake among those who either hate how money corrupts, or hate that they don't have any. Nowhere in the Bible can you find "money is the root of all evil." On the other hand, the Apostle Paul said, "The <u>love</u> of money is the root of all evil." So technically, having money isn't nearly the problem that loving (or worshipping) the almighty buck is. (1 Tim. 6:10)

A: (b) Paul and his companions were on a ship being tossed around on the ocean. (Acts 27:27–30)

A: (a) Speaking in tongues is considered a gift of the Holy Spirit that enables the believer to speak in a language not familiar to that individual. Paul suggested that people who have this gift should also pray for God to grant them the ability to understand (or self-interpret) what they are saying. (1 Cor. 14:13)

A: (b) Lepers. (Lev. 13:45) We do, however, love the visual of a *lawyer* with *leprosy* who happens to be a *harlot* caught in *adultery* walking around town shouting *"Unclean!"*

Q: Unscramble this famous Bible quotation:
witness your false shall not you neighbor bear
against

Q: In which book of the Bible can the above quote
be found?
(a) Genesis   (b) Exodus   (c) Leviticus

Q: What famous biblical character was most
closely associated with Tarshish, Joppa, and
Nineveh?

Q: What two apostles were put into prison in
Jerusalem for preaching the gospel?
(a) Jesus and Peter
(b) Peter, Paul, and Mary
(c) Paul and Barnabas
(d) John and Peter

A: "You shall not bear false witness against your neighbor."

A: (b) Exodus 20:16.

A: Jonah. Trying to run away from the job God had for him, Jonah headed for Tarshish, but ended up in Joppa. From there he hopped a ship bound for Tarshish, but God caught up with him and caused a massive storm. In order to calm the waters, Jonah volunteered to be tossed out of the ship. From there, he got swallowed by a whale and then spewed up onto land. Finally Jonah gets the message and goes to Nineveh to do what God has told him to do. Some of us learn harder than others. (Jon. 1:1)

A: (d) Documented in Acts 4:3, John and Peter found themselves locked up in Jerusalem. Both were confronted by their accusers but boldly refused to yield in their proclamation that Jesus was Lord. Confused and fearful of a potential uprising by citizens who were being converted, their captors allowed them to leave Jerusalem.

Q: What unfaithful Old Testament woman had children named Lo-ruhamah, Lo-ammi, and Jazreel?

Q: Which of the following foods are never mentioned in the Bible?
   (a) locust   (b) pumpkins
   (c) cucumbers   (d) melons

Q: Which of the following is not one of the fruits of the spirit?
   (a) tolerance   (b) love
   (c) peace   (d) kindness
   (e) self-control

Q: Which of the following birds is never mentioned in the Bible?
   (a) bats   (b) eagles
   (c) storks   (d) parrots

A: Gomer, (no relation to Pyle, USMC) wife of the prophet Hosea. (Hos. 1)

A: (b) Hope it won't ruin your dinner to know that John the Baptist frequently enjoyed locust, especially when dipped in honey. Pumpkins are native to North America and therefore would not have been found in scripture.

A: (a) Tolerance is not on the list found in Galatians 5.

A: (d) Surprise! Parrots are never mentioned in the Bible. Most of you probably guessed (a) bats, but you'd be wrong since they're mentioned in Isaiah 2:20. Apparently the Hebrews classified bats as birds simply because they fly.

Q: Which of the following characters is not found
in the New Testament?
(a) Jethro   (b) Judas
(c) John   (d) James

Q: Which of the following prophets doesn't
belong?
(a) Elijah   (b) Malachi
(c) Moloch   (d) Agabus

Q: Which of the following names is never used to
describe the Devil in the Bible?
(a) prince of demons   (b) prince of darkness
(c) the tempter   (d) father of lies

A: (a) Jethro, Moses' father-in-law, is an Old Testament guy and is not mentioned in the New Testament.

A: (c) Sorry, but Mr. Moloch was no prophet, in fact he was a god (small "g") of the Ammonites.

A: (b) Satan answers to bunches of names throughout the Bible, but "prince of darkness" is not one of them.

Q: In 2 Kings 2:24, we find good old Elisha minding his own business when a "group of youths" confronts him with the taunt "baldhead." How did Elisha respond?
(a) he did nothing, as he was a man of God
(b) he beat them with his staff
(c) he threw his hair piece at them
(d) he asked God to send two bears to maul them

Q: Who advised husbands and wives not to go overboard when it comes to sexual abstinence, because it could lead to temptation?
(a) Jesus   (b) God
(c) Masters & Johnson   (d) Paul

Q: Which of Paul's followers did he refer to as a "man of God"?
(a) Timothy   (b) Barnabas
(c) Beelzebub   (d) Titus

A: (d) You guessed it! Cue the bears! God obliged and sent two bears, which mauled forty-two of the little hoodlums. It should be pointed out that the original Hebrew translation describes these "youths" in such a manner as to indicate they were more like juvenile delinquents or young criminals than good-natured kids out for a laugh.

A: (d) Paul made this helpful admonition. (1 Cor. 7:5)

A: (a) Timothy. (1 Tim. 6:11)

Q: Who referred to Jesus as a "man of God"?

Q: What sort of lips are "an abomination" to God?
(a) chapped   (b) lying
(c) loose   (d) gossiping

Q: What do you call a person who goes out of his way to help someone?

Q: To those who claim the Bible is flawed, which apostle claimed all Scripture to be "God-breathed"?

Q: What organization likely placed a Bible in your hotel nightstand?

Q: How many church buildings are mentioned the Bible?

A: No one, which isn't too shocking since Jesus, according to the New Testament, <u>was</u> God in the flesh.

A: (b) Lying. (Prov. 12:22)

A: A Good Samaritan, based on the parable Jesus told of the Samaritan who helped the beaten traveler while the religious people passed by and gave no aid. (Luke 10:29)

A: Paul certified this in his letter to Timothy. (2 Tim. 3:16) Some Bible translations have used the word "inspired" instead of "God-breathed," though in fact "God-breathed" is an exact translation of the original Greek wording.

A: The Gideons, who have been giving away free Bibles since 1898.

A: None. Jesus and His disciples did not have, and some believe did not want, special buildings for worship. Instead, they met in homes, or wherever a group of believers gathered.

Q: Who tore a lion apart with his bare hands?
(Hint—six letters)

Q: From the "kiss and tell" files: Who told his
mistress "all his heart" and wound up losing his
hair, eyesight, and life?

Q: Scotland is home to a city that is supposedly the
birthplace of the game of golf. What apostle is
the town named for?

Q: Which Bible translation does the abbreviation
TLB refer to?

Q: King David could party! What wife of King
David scolded him big time for dancing in the
streets and exposing himself?

A: Most people believe it was Daniel since he was thrown to the lions, but it was Samson who accomplished this feat. (Judg. 14:5–6)

A: Samson made the mistake of spilling his guts to that evil-doer Delilah in Judges 16.

A: The town is St. Andrews, named of course, after Andrew. Andrew was Peter's brother and one of the two fishermen recruited by Jesus. It was at the sea of Galilee that Jesus uttered to Andrew and Simon the famous Christian verse, "Come, follow me, and I will make you fishers of men." (Matt. 4:18–19)

A: There are many Bible translations, but TLB refers to The Living Bible, which was first introduced in 1976.

A: Michal. David tried to explain that his spontaneous joy was because the Ark of the Covenant had been returned to the Israelites, but Michal wasn't buying it. (2 Sam. 6:16–20)

Q: Owie! Who made a gift of two hundred Philistine foreskins to his future father-in-law?

Q: What king had a curious dream of seven fatted cows being eaten by seven skinny cows?

Q: What Old Testament character is best described as "wise, witty, brilliant, and clever"?

Q: What king received seventy human heads in baskets?

A: David. (1 Sam. 18:27) King Saul didn't like the idea of David marrying his daughter Michal so he told him that he would only consent to the marriage if David forked-over the foreskins. Saul's plan all along was that David would be killed trying to get the goods. Imagine King Saul's surprise when David not only accepted the challenge, but succeeded—much to the chagrin of 200 Philistines. Apparently "just say no" wasn't a common phrase back then.

A: The pharaoh of Egypt dreamt this dream, which was later interpreted by Joseph in Genesis 41. By the way, the dream meant that there was a seven-year famine on the way and that pharaoh should store up food and supplies for the hard times ahead.

A: Solomon.

A: King Jehu. Keeping your head about you while all around you are losing theirs was a bit of a challenge in the Old Testament, especially if you were a member of King Ahab's family. While in the city of Jezreel, King Jehu put to death all of Ahab's family, friends, and court. (2 Kings 10:7)

Q: What author of a book in the Bible was prone to an upset tummy?

Q: Who was the Old Testament guy with a real "killer" attitude (Hint: His name begins with the letter "C")

Q: Abraham's wife got a real kick out of hearing something. In fact she laughed hysterically when she found out she was _____.
(a) dirt poor   (b) pregnant
(c) a prophetess   (d) the new queen

Q: When Sarah had their baby, Abraham had a small problem too. What was his problem?
(a) he was deceased   (b) he was 100
(c) he was divorced   (d) he was a leper

A: Timothy was notorious for a queazy stomach, which is why his good friend and spiritual mentor, Paul, suggested he take a little wine for his ailment. (1 Tim. 5:23)

A: Cain, who murdered his brother Abel, of course. (Gen. 4:8)

A: (b) Sarah was *(gulp)* 90 years old when God decided it was time for her to have a baby. (Gen. 18:10–12)

A: (b) Good old Abraham was 100 years old when Sarah bore Isaac. Probably not many games of catch going on between Abraham and his son. (Gen. 21:5)

It's the Gospel

Q: Jesus sent this man fishing in order to get money for taxes.
   (a) Paul   (b) Silas
   (c) Charlie the Tuna   (d) Peter

Q: Which of Jesus' disciples was in charge of the group's money?

Q: "If thou wilt be perfect, go and sell what thou has, and give to the poor." Jesus said these words to what biblical character?

Q: Let's test your knowledge of biblical money. In only one area of scripture is a coin's appearance referred to. Whose face was on it?
   (a) Susan B. Anthony   (b) King Agrippa
   (c) King Solomon   (d) Caesar

A: (d) Peter. (Matt.17:24–27)

A: From the "seemed like a good idea at the time" file, Judas was in charge of the group's money. (John 13:29)

A: Jesus said this to the rich young man who had done many things according to Jesus, but realized he still lacked something. What he lacked was a complete faith and trust in Jesus Christ and his wealth was apparently a barrier. (Matt. 19:21)

A: (d) Jesus, in his conversation with the Pharisees, mentioned that Caesar's face appeared on the Roman coin. You may recall that the Pharisees were trying to trap Jesus into an argument that would allow them to condemn Him. (Matt. 22:18–22)

Q: Peter found something very strange in the mouth of a fish. What was it?
(a) a coin   (b) a pen
(c) Jonah   (d) a sword

Q: In which of Jesus' parables did the servants receive money to invest?
(a) talents   (b) the rich young man
(c) sowing and reaping   (d) saver

Q: What well-known biblical character squandered his money on prostitutes?

Q: Which of the following is not one of Jesus' parables?
(a) the blind man and the donkey
(b) the Good Samaritan
(c) the lost sheep

A: (a) A coin. To be exact, it was a four-drachma coin. Jesus told Peter to cast his line into the water and to take his first catch, open its mouth, and find the coin. This coin was to be used to pay the customary taxes. (Matt. 17:27)

A: (a) The parable of the talents was how Jesus taught young believers how to use wisely the spiritual gifts God has given them. (Matt. 25:14–30)

A: It was the Prodigal Son (from Jesus' parable of the same name). (Luke 15:30)

A: (a) Sorry…no blind men and donkeys, but we all agree Jesus could have made a great story out of it.

Q: Which of these biblical towns did Jesus <u>not</u> visit?
   (a) Nazareth   (b) Jerusalem
   (c) Jericho   (d) Corinth

Q: What wealthy man buried Jesus in his own tomb?
   (a) Joseph   (b) Paul
   (c) Lazarus   (d) Pilate

Q: To whom were the wise men speaking when they said, "We have seen his star in the east, and are going to worship him"?
   (a) their camels   (b) God
   (c) Herod   (d) Mary, Jesus' mother

Q: What happened at the precise moment when the sun darkened and the curtain in the temple was torn in two?
   (a) Jesus died   (b) God wept
   (c) Jesus was born

A: (d) Many believe Jericho to be the answer because it is more closely associated with the Old Testament, but the correct answer is *Corinth*, in Greece. This was the city Paul visited and is the focus of Paul's letter to the Corinthians.

A: (a) His name was Joseph of Arimathea and he was a disciple of Jesus. In biblical times it was not unusual for rich men to purchase burial caves in anticipation of their death. Joseph went to Pilate and received permission to take Jesus' body, prepare Him for burial, and place Him in his burial cave. (Mark 15:43)

A: (c) King Herod. Little did they know that Herod would plot to follow them to Jesus to have the newborn Christ killed. (Matt. 2:2)

A: (a) Jesus died.

Q: What did Jesus use to drive the money-changers out of the temple?
   (a) tax collectors   (b) snakes
   (c) a whip   (d) a rod and staff

Q: What two sisters had a brother named Lazarus and were close friends of Jesus?

Q: What do giving sight to the blind, making the lame walk, and turning water to wine have in common?

Q: Who fasted for forty days and forty nights?
   (a) Jesus   (b) Paul
   (c) Moses   (d) Judas
   (e) Jonah

Q: Do the Gospels trace Jesus' genealogy through Joseph or through Mary?

A: (c) A whip. Yes, Jesus could get angry when it was called for. He made a whip out of cords and drove the money-changers out of the temple. Next, He overturned tables and scattered their coins. An angry Jesus was quoted as saying, "How dare you turn my Father's house into a market!" (Mark 11:15)

A: Mary and Martha. (Luke 10:38–42; John 11)

A: They were each miracles performed by Jesus.

A: (a) and (c). Jesus is the easy answer as He fasted in order to withstand the temptation of Satan. (Matt. 4:2) But how many of you recalled that Moses also went without food or drink for forty days while he was in the Lord's presence? (Deut. 9:9)

A: Through Joseph, as the Jewish custom at the time was to trace descent through the male, and never the female side of the family. (Luke 3:23; Matt. 1:16)

Q: In the parable in which a man calls on his friend at midnight, what was the man asking to borrow?
(a) NyQuil®
(b) wine
(c) bread
(d) blankets

Q: Which rotten and evil king, appointed to his post by the Romans, ordered the massacre of all the male babies in Bethlehem?
(a) Herod
(b) Pilate
(c) Caesar
(d) Old King Cole

Q: Who said "Lord, save me!" as he learned that walking on water was tougher than it appeared?

Q: What approximate time was it when Peter took his eye off Jesus and began to drown?
(a) afternoon
(b) midday
(c) evening
(d) early morning

A: (c) Three loaves of bread. This is the parable in which Jesus admonishes his disciples to "ask, and you shall receive; seek, and you shall find; knock, and the door will be opened up to you." (Luke 11:5)

A: (a) Herod (oddly known in history books as "Herod the Great") planned the massacre as a way of rooting-out and eliminating the newborn Christ. Bad man... bad plan...bad consequences. (Matt. 2:13–18)

A: Peter. You may recall that Peter actually succeeded in walking a short distance on the water, but as the wind picked up, he began to panic and took his eyes off of Jesus. Once this happened, he began to sink like a stone. The moral of the story is that believers can do all things if they keep their eye on Jesus. (Matt. 14:30)

A: (d) All accounts place this event during what is called the "fourth watch," which places it between 3:00 AM and 6:00 AM. (Matt. 14:30)

Q: Who did Jesus say will "wail" and "gnash" their teeth as they are tossed into the furnace of fire?
(a) politicians   (b) wicked people
(c) unbelievers

Q: Which disciple cut off a servant's ear while trying to protect Jesus?
(a) Judas   (b) Gillette
(c) Matthew   (d) Peter

Q: Among the following, whom did Jesus _not_ heal?
(a) a man with dropsy   (b) a deaf mute
(c) a servant's nose

Q: How long was Jonah in the belly of the great fish?

Q: Who entered Judas' heart to urge him to turn against Jesus?
(a) demons   (b) Satan
(c) the media   (d) Pilate

A: (b). Although some might say (a) would make a tremendous pay-per-view event. (Matt. 13:50)

A: (d) Peter drew his sword as he prepared to defend Jesus to the death. To everyone's surprise, Jesus calmly picked-up the detached ear and returned it to the servant's head—fully healed. (John 18:10)

A: (c) Nose jobs weren't in vogue at the time.

A: Three days and three nights. (Matt. 12:40)

A: (b) Judas dropped his spiritual guard long enough for Satan to infiltrate and influence him to turn against Jesus.

Q: Jesus said, "Get behind Me, Satan" to Peter because Peter refused to accept Jesus' prediction. What did Jesus predict?
   (a) The Miracle Mets of '69
   (b) His own death and resurrection
   (c) Judas' betrayal of Jesus
   (d) Peter's own violent death

Q: Which parable of Jesus features a rich man in hell, begging for a few drops of water to cool his tongue?

Q: Fill in the blanks: Jesus said, "Go into the village opposite you, and immediately you will find a _____ tied, and a _____ with her."

Q: Why did four men lower their friend through the roof to be healed by Jesus?

A: (b) You might imagine the mental anguish Peter had in trying to deal with the prophecy of Jesus' death and resurrection. (Matt. 16:21)

A: The parable of the rich man and Lazarus the beggar should serve as a warning to all who worship money! (Luke 16:24)

A: *Donkey* and *colt*. Jesus was well aware of the prophecy stating He would ride into Jerusalem for his impending crucifixion on a donkey. His disciples went into Jerusalem, found the donkey and colt in the exact location Jesus had told them to look, and returned with them. (Matt. 21:2)

A: The room was so crowded that the four men knew they could never get inside with their friend to be healed by Jesus. Lowering him through the roof allowed Jesus to heal him. (Mark 2:4)

Q: What was the illness suffered by the man
lowered through the roof by his four friends?
(a) acrophobia   (b) paralysis
(c) leprosy

Q: The man from Gadara (Mark 5:2) made his
dwelling in the tombs because...
(a) he had an unclean spirit
(b) he was demon possessed
(c) he was a social outcast
(d) he was in the "can I get a witness"
protection program

Q: No one had been able to capture the demon
possessed man from Gadara. Why?

A: (b) Scripture states the man was suffering from paralysis. In case you were wondering, acrophobia is the fear of heights. Had it been the correct answer it would have been the first documented case of a clinical practice called "aversion therapy" whereby people are confronted by their worst fears. (Mark 2:3–4)

A: (a) and (b). A bit of a trick since both are scripturally interchangeable expressions meaning "the man was possessed."

A: It wasn't that demon-possessed men were particularly fast or hard to catch. It was just that no chains were strong enough to bind the man. Each time the townspeople would chain him up, the demons would give him the strength to break free. Apparently this was a very common practice. (Mark 5:4)

Q: Where did Jesus send the demons after he sent
them out of the possessed man?
(a) into politics
(b) into a herd of donkeys
(c) into a herd of swine
(d) into a dark valley

Q: Jesus healed a woman afflicted with a
"hemorrhage for twelve years," who had
suffered greatly at the hands of which of the
following?
(a) HMOs   (b) Pharisees
(c) physicians   (d) magicians

Q: In the story of how Jesus fed the five thousand
who had come to see him, who actually did the
serving?

Q: True or False? After feeding the five thousand,
Jesus sent the disciples ahead in a boat while He
healed the few left behind.

A: (c) Jesus sent the demons into a herd of swine who were feeding together in a nearby field. Upon receiving the demons, the swine ran into and drowned in a lake. (Mark 5:13)

A: (c) Possibly stricken with a form of hemophilia, the physicians of that time could do little or nothing to help this woman, though they had apparently done much to cause her pain. (Mark 5:26)

A: Scripture tells us Jesus' disciples fed the five thousand. Scripture reinforces the fact that the disciples served the meals as it states that the disciples also gathered the twelve baskets after the people were done eating. (Mark 6:41)

A: False. According to Mark 6:45, Jesus sent his disciples ahead so He could spend some time kneeling in prayer before His father.

Q: How long did Jesus pray before deciding who
would be His twelve disciples?
(a) all night   (b) without end
(c) through lunch   (d) 30 days

Q: What is the name of the parable about the man
who went down from Jerusalem to Jerico and
was stripped and beaten by thieves?

Q: One of Jesus' disciples asked Him, "Lord, teach
us to pray, as John also taught his disciples."
What famous answer did Jesus give?
(a) The Sinner's Prayer
(b) The Lord's Prayer
(c) The Perfect Prayer

Q: When Peter saw Jesus walking on water he
thought he was seeing a ghost. To prove that
Jesus was real, Peter asked Him to do
something. What was it?

A: (a) All night. (Mark 8:8)

A: The parable of the Good Samaritan. Jesus used this parable to illustrate how hypocritical the upright and seemingly religious people were as they avoided the poor beaten man at the side of the road. Whereas the Samaritan, a people from the town of Samaria who were looked down upon as having low character, stopped and looked after the traveler. (Luke 10:30–36)

A: (b) Jesus taught them The Lord's Prayer found in Luke 11:2–4. "Father, hallowed be your name, your kingdom come. Give us each day our daily bread. Forgive us our sins, for we also forgive everyone who sins against us. And lead us not into temptation."

A: According to Matthew 14:28, Peter said, "Lord, if it is You, command me to come to You on the water."

Q: Jesus said, "A prophet without honor in his own country and in his own house." What does this famous quote refer to?

Q: Jesus told one of His disciples, "I will give you the keys to _____."
(a) the city   (b) life
(c) the kingdom of heaven   (d) the car

Q: What pierced Jesus' side so that blood and water flowed out?

Q: Who washed his hands to show he was innocent of shedding Jesus' blood?
(a) Pilate   (b) the Centurion
(c) Caiaphas   (d) Judas

Q: "Sweating blood" is a biblical term commonly used today. Who was it that "sweated blood" in the Bible and what did the phrase mean?

A: It was Jesus' response as to why the people of His own city didn't acknowledge or pay Him the respect He was due. (Matt. 13:57)

A: (c) According to Matthew 16:18–19, this promise was based on Peter's confession of faith in Jesus as the Christ.

A: The Bible documents how a Roman soldier lanced Jesus' side as he hung motionless on the cross. This was actually a typical Roman procedure used to determine if the crucified was dead or not depending on how much blood flowed from the wound. (John 19:34)

A: (a) Pilate was a weasel. On one hand he did his part to condemn Jesus to death while on the other, he decided he didn't want to be held responsible on the off chance Jesus actually was the Son of God. (Matt. 27:24)

A: This graphic phrase was used only once in the Bible. Luke (the physician apostle) used it to describe literally how blood came out of Jesus' pores like sweat as He prayed in Gethsemane. Jesus' prayer concerned His crucifixion and petition to God the Father whether He truly had to go through with this brutal fate. (Luke 22:44)

Q: When nasty old King Herod had a birthday, he gave a gift to his wife's daughter. What was the gift?
(a) John the Baptist's head
(b) Peter's head
(c) her own mother's head

Q: What was the name of Horodias' daughter (Herod's niece) who asked for the head of John the Baptist?
(a) Herod extra dry   (b) Herodette
(c) Hereodite   (d) None of the above

Q: Two Old Testament characters appeared on the Mount of Transfiguration with Jesus. One was Elijah, and Charlton Heston later depicted the other.

A: (a) Oh what a tangled web. You see, King Herod had married his brother's wife Herodias. (How's that for a coincidence?) John the Baptist had condemned this marriage as scripturally wrong, which really ticked off Herodias. So Herod had John arrested. Then, at the birthday party, Herod told his niece he would grant her any wish she desired. Being a chip-off-the-old-block, she demanded the head of John the Baptist. Although more than a little troubled by her request, Herod nonetheless acquiesced. (Matt. 14:3–11)

A: (d) The Bible doesn't divulge the girl's name. With a mother named Herodias and a step-father/uncle named Herod, we could only assume a focus group would have been needed to name the girl. She is only referred to as "daughter" and "the girl." (Matt. 14:8)

A: Holy Moses. For Charlton's sake we hope you got this one. (Matt. 17:3)

Q: Jesus said someone would sit at His right and left hands in heaven. Whom did He identify?
   (a) Peter and Paul
   (b) Manny and Moe
   (c) Jesus never discusses this
   (d) those for whom the Father prepares those places

Q: What did a woman do to Jesus at the house of Simon the leper in Bethany?

Q: Unscramble this famous Bible quotation: loved for God the world only Son begotten so that He gave

Q: In which book of the Bible can the above quote be found?
   (a) John   (b) James   (c) Jude

Q: True or False? The chief priests offered Judas Iscariot a reward for betraying Jesus.

A: (c) Jesus was approached by James' and Johns' mother who asked Jesus to allow each of her sons to sit at His right and left hand in heaven. Jesus told her that it was not His decision, but His Father's. (Matt. 20:23)

A: This was the story of a woman who brought expensive perfumed oil to Jesus and poured it over his head. The disciples were indignant that she wasted something that they could have sold to feed the poor. Jesus told them that they will always have the poor to help, but that she was merely preparing Him for burial, which He knew was close at hand. (Matt. 26:7–12)

A: "For God so loved the world that he gave His only begotten Son."

A: (a) John 3:16.

A: False. The betrayal was initiated by Judas, not the chief priests. (Matt. 26:14–15)

Q: What did Judas receive from the chief priests for betraying Jesus?
(a) a washer and dryer set   (b) 20 silver coins
(c) 30 silver coins

Q: Jesus predicted Peter would do something three times. What was His prediction?

Q: What sign did Judas use to identify and betray Jesus to those sent to arrest Him?
(a) a pink ribbon   (b) a kiss
(c) a hug   (d) a secret handshake

Q: There were two men crucified next to Jesus. They were described as _____?
(a) journalists   (b) criminals
(c) innocent men   (d) victims

Q: This man went to Pilate and asked for Jesus' body after he had died on the cross. Who was he? (Hint: It was a familiar name to Jesus)

A: (c) 30 silver coins, which he would later throw away in self-disgust before committing suicide. (Matt. 27:3)

A: Jesus predicted that, after His arrest, Peter would be confronted by the authorities, looking for any and all who were involved with Jesus. Jesus correctly predicted that Peter would deny knowing Him three times. (Matt. 26:34)

A: (b) The prearranged signal between Judas and Jesus' accusers was for Judas to identify Jesus by simply kissing Him on the cheek. (Matt. 26:48)

A: (b) Criminals, although in some Bible translations they are referred to as "thieves." It is unknown if they were also journalists. (Matt. 27:38)

A: His name was Joseph of Arimathea (not Joseph His father) and out of kindness he had Jesus buried in an expensive cave tomb he had purchased for himself. (Matt. 27:57–58)

Q: Who rolled back the stone from the door of Jesus' tomb?

    (a) thieves   (b) Mary and Martha

    (c) an angel   (d) Jesus Himself

Q: Where did Jesus arrange to meet His disciples after His resurrection?

    (a) heaven   (b) Starbucks

    (c) Galilee   (d) Bethlehem

Q: How many days was Jesus tempted by Satan? (Hint: The temptation took much longer than the Gospels seem to indicate)

Q: What was the first miracle Jesus performed?

    (a) turning water into wine

    (b) healing multiple sicknesses

    (c) feeding 5000

    (d) turning pigs into Sizzlean

A: (c) An angel who was present in the tomb when Mary Magdalene and the other Mary entered the tomb is most often credited with moving the huge stone. The angel said, "I know that you are looking for Jesus who as been crucified. He is not here, for He has risen." (Matt. 28:2-8)

A: (c) Galilee. No credit awarded for guessing they met at the Starbucks at the corner of Wilshire and Ninth in Galilee. (Matt. 20:10)

A: 40 days. This is a fascinating passage of scripture where we find Jesus, led by the Holy Spirit, into the wilderness to be tempted by Satan. Jesus endured temptation as a man (and not the Son of God) relying on His faith in God's wisdom to withstand everything Satan threw at Him. (Matt. 4:1)

A: (b) It is believed to have been performed while Jesus was on His way to Galilee. This is where a "large number" of Syrians came to Him to be healed of a multitude of afflictions including diseases, pains, demons, epilepsy, and paralysis. (Matt. 5:23-25; Mark 7:26))

Bible Potpourri

(Each of the following 14 questions asks you to name the biblical character. Each name contains five letters.)

Q: Who was the only apostle we know for sure was married?

Q: What strange "cat" kept Paul in prison, hoping he would try to bribe him for his release?

Q: What holy man was anointed by an immoral woman?

Q: Which "Li'l" cousin of Saul was commander of the king's troops?

Q: Who was caught in such a violent storm at sea that he didn't see the sun or the stars for many days?
   (a) Jonah   (b) Noah
   (c) Jesus   (d) Paul

A: Peter, who is mentioned as having a mother-in-law. Therefore we can deduce that he also had a wife. (Mark 1:30)

A: Felix (get the "cat" reference now?). (Acts 24:26)

A: Jesus. A woman who had lived a "sinful life" came to Jesus while He was sitting at the table in a Pharisee's house. She had an alabaster jar of perfume that she used to anoint His feet. This infuriated the Pharisee who believed Jesus should have never let a sinful person anoint His feet. Jesus went on to explain how faith and belief overcome all sin. (Luke 7:37–38)

A: Abner. Hence the hint "Li'l" from the cartoon character Li'l Abner. (1 Sam. 14:50)

A: (d) An argument can be made that since Jonah was in the whale for days, he could possibly be the correct answer, but the Bible tells us that Paul spent many days in a violent sea on his way to preach the Word in Crete. (Acts 27:20)

Q: Who was the first apostle to be martyred?

Q: What businesswoman was baptized by Paul and Silas?

Q: What apostle, a traveling companion of Paul, was sometimes called Silvanus?

Q: Who cursed a fig tree for not bearing fruit?

A: James. And in case you didn't know, James is Jesus'
    blood and birth brother. (Gal. 1:19)

A: Lydia, who is described as a woman from Thyatira
    who sold purple fabrics and was a worshipper of God.
    Note: Purple fabrics were highly valued and generally
    accessible only to the affluent for the reason that
    purple dyes were hard to come by. The rarity of these
    fabrics implies that Lydia must have been an
    influential businesswoman for her time. (Acts
    16:14–15)

A: Silas (which is apparently short for Silvanus) was a
    constant companion of Paul and Timothy as they
    spread the Good News about Jesus. (1 Thess. 1:1)

A: Apparently Jesus and Peter came across a barren fig
    tree. Jesus cursed (not profanity) the tree for not
    producing fruit. A short time later, they passed the fig
    tree again and Peter noticed that the tree had
    withered. Jesus, of course, used this as a lesson about
    faith and belief. (Mark 11:21)

Q: Who, according to tradition, wrote the book of Psalms?

Q: Who told his followers they would have the power to handle deadly snakes?

Q: According to Peter, what person is like a ravenous lion?

Q: What Old Testament prophet had his shade-producing vine eaten by a worm?

A: King David, Asaph (a priest who headed the service of music), and others. Psalms is the largest and perhaps most widely used book in the Bible. Its 150 songs addresses such diverse topics such as jubilation, war, peace, worship, judgment, prophecy, praise, and lament.

A: Jesus. This is part of a conversation that took place between Jesus (after His resurrection) and the eleven apostles. In this scripture, Jesus instructs them to go out and preach the gospel without fear. He had empowered and sheltered the apostles against harm—including the drinking of poison and handling of deadly snakes. (Mark 16:18)

A: Satan. Peter is cautioning believers to be on guard as their adversary, the devil, prowls around like a roaring lion, seeking someone to devour. (1 Pet. 5:8)

A: Jonah. This is a wonderful passage in scripture illustrating the great lengths God will go to grab the attention of someone who is trying to ignore Him. (Jon. 4:7)

Q: Whose wives included Abigail, Michal, Maacah, Haggith, Eglah, and Bathsheba?

*(The following do not necessarily
have five letter answers)*

Q: We all know that the baby Jesus was given gifts of gold, frankincense, and myrrh. What is frankincense?
(a) foot-long hot dogs   (b) incense
(c) oil for lamps   (d) perfume

Q: What two Old Testament men were with Jesus when a shining cloud covered them?

Q: Which of these animals is never mentioned in the Bible?
(a) hyena   (b) tiger
(c) leopard   (d) fox

A: David. (2 Sam. 12:8)

A: (b) Incense. Frankincense is a vegetable or tree resin that is burnt to produce a strong odor. It was often used in sacrificial fumigation.

A: Moses and Elijah. (Matt.17:15)

A: (c) *Leopards* will lie in wait (Jer. 5:6), *fox* will climb on buildings (Neh. 4:3), and *hyenas* will howl (Isa. 13:22), but *tigers* are nowhere to be found in the Bible.

Q: Who, out of the following list of saintly biblical women, doesn't belong:
Mary Magdalene, Ruth, Lydia, Jezebel

Q: Which of the twelve disciples was the "disciple whom Jesus loved"?
(a) Judas   (b) Peter
(c) Andrew   (d) John

Q: "Lead us not into temptation" is a famous line from The Lord's Prayer. What line follows?

Q: Unscramble this famous Bible quotation:
Way the the truth the life am I and the

Q: In which book of the Bible can the above quote be found?
(a) Joel   (b) Judges   (c) John

A: Mary, Ruth, and Lydia were profound women of character and faith. Jezebel, on the other hand, was a wicked queen in the Old Testament.

A: (d) Most Christians mistakenly believe the answer to be Peter. The references to Jesus loving a disciple, however, are found in the Gospels of John. Scholars believe it was John himself who was the disciple Jesus loved, but that modesty prevented him from naming himself. (John 13:23; 19:26; 20:2; 21:7)

A: … but deliver us from evil. (Matt. 6:13)

A: "I am the way, the truth, and the life."

A: (c) John 14:6.

Q: Though the New Testament was written in Greek, what was the basic language used throughout the Roman Empire?
  (a) Hebrew   (b) Greek
  (c) Ebonics   (d) Latin

Q: Let's say you look outside tonight and the moon is "blood red." What is likely happening?
  (a) the sixth seal has been broken
  (b) it's corn planting season
  (c) the apocalypse is at hand
  (d) end days prophecy is being fulfilled

Q: According to the New Testament, what cleanses us from all sin?

Q: Who played the role of David in the 1951 classic movie *David and Bathsheba*?
  (a) Walter Brennan   (b) John Wayne
  (c) Don Knotts   (d) Gregory Peck

A: (d) Gregory Peck. If you're really a movie buff, you'll recall that his Bathsheba was the lovely and talented Susan Hayward.

A: (d) Latin.

A: (a), (c), and (d). This is the sixth sign in the book of Revelation 6:12, which signifies that the apocalypse is upon the earth. You may plant your corn if you wish, but it would amount to the biblical equivalent to realigning the deck chairs on the *Titanic*.

A: The Blood of Christ. This is the foundation of the grace and forgiveness principles of the New Testament. Theologically Christ shed blood and died for our sins. Because He already paid the ultimate price, your sins are cleansed when you: (1) accept Christ, (2) repent from your sins, and (3) ask Jesus for forgiveness.

A: (d) Gregory Peck. If you're really a movie buff, you'll recall that his Bathsheba was the lovely and talented Susan Hayward.

Q: Let's say you lived in the time of Moses and you found that your wife was unclean or full of sin. According to the laws of Moses, what could you do?
(a) divorce her   (b) sell her
(c) whip her   (d) call her bad names

Q: In Hebrew, what does the word Jerusalem mean?
(a) peace   (b) land of God
(c) holiness   (d) land of strife

Q: What Greek city was well-known as a den of sin?
(a) Thessalonia   (b) Corinth
(c) Malta   (d) Sodom

Q: What book of the New Testament bears the same name as a Roman emperor?
(a) Timothy   (b) Peter
(c) Titus   (d) Caesar

A: (a) According to the laws of Moses, you were given the option of divorcing an unclean wife. (Deut. 24:1)

A: (a) Ironically enough, it means peace.

A: (b) Corinth. You may have guessed (d) Sodom, as it was certainly a den of sin, but Sodom was not a Greek city. Before God leveled Sodom, it is believed to have been somewhere bordering the Great Sea in the Kingdom of Israel.

A: (c) Titus.

Q: What controversial rock opera of the 1980s ends with Jesus' crucifixion and not his resurrection?

Q: What popular rock opera is about Jacob and his twelve sons?

Q: In all of Shakespeare's plays, only one biblical character is portrayed in a role. Can you name that character?

Q: In the novel *Moby Dick*, what was the name of the character who tried to warn Ishmael not to sail on Captain Ahab's ship? (Hint: The character's name is also that of an Old Testament prophet)

Q: True or False? Many Christians lift their hands up in praise to God during worship. Although flattering to their belief principles, this practice has no foundation in the Bible.

A: *Jesus Christ Superstar* by Andrew Lloyd Webber and Tim Rice.

A: *Joseph and the Amazing Technicolor Dreamcoat.*

A: Octavius in *Julius Caesar*. Octavius was better known as Augustus Caesar, who is mentioned in the Gospel of Luke. (Luke 2:1)

A: Elijah.

A: False. It's called "lifting up holy hands" and it's an outward sign of the moving of the Holy Spirit within the believer. References are seen in Psalms 134:2 and in 1 Timothy 2:8.

Q: "Father, Son, and Holy Spirit" are common words heard during prayer and worship. Oddly enough, they are mentioned together only once in a New Testament book. Which one?
(a) Matthew   (b) Isaiah
(c) Psalms   (d) James

Q: Who irritated his brothers by telling them of his dreams?
(a) Joseph   (b) Daniel
(c) Jacob   (d) The Amazing Kreskin

Q: Paul's first traveling companion was Barnabas. Who was his second?
(a) Silas   (b) Timothy
(c) a demon   (d) Philip

Q: Who is the most mentioned woman in the Bible?
(a) Mary   (b) Mary Magdalene
(c) Sarah   (d) Delilah

A: (a) In the book referred to as Jesus' great commission, Jesus tells the disciples to baptize in the name of the Father, of the Son, and of the Spirit. (Matt. 28:19) (By the way, Psalms and Isaiah are Old Testament books.)

A: (a) Joseph. All three (minus Kreskin) are associated with dreams and dream interpretation in the Bible; only Joseph got himself into big trouble and ultimately sold into slavery for sharing his dreams with his brothers. (Gen. 37:5)

A: (a) Silas. Paul chose Silas to accompany him through Syria and Cilicia after a sharp dispute between him and John (called Mark). The dispute was over Paul's belief that John abandoned them during an earlier sojourn. You will rest better in knowing that Paul and John patched up their differences. (Acts 15:36–41)

A: (c) One would have believed that the birth mother of Jesus would have received the most honorable mentions, however neither of the two Marys nor our scissor-bearing friend are mentioned as often as Sarah (56 times).

Q: Who had the only known case of halitosis in the Bible?
(a) Jonah (b) Ishmael
(c) Job (d) Satan

Q: Whose wife was turned into a pillar of salt?
(a) Lot's wife (b) Paul's wife
(c) Abraham's wife

Q: According to the Book of Job, what sort of man has a fat neck and a bulging waistline?
(a) a couch potato (b) a sluggard
(c) a wicked man (d) a sinful man

Q: What year was the New King James Version of the Bible first published?
(a) 20 BC (b) 1501
(c) 1982 (d) 1912

A: (c) What did you expect with a diet of locust? Job was troubled that his wife found his breath to be "offensive" or "strange," depending on the Bible translation. (Job 19:17)

A: (a) Lot strongly admonished his wife to not look back at the cities of Sodom and Gomorrah as the Lord rained sulphur down on them. Either forgetting, or discounting the warning, she turned and gazed upon the cities and was turned into a 4'11" salt lick. (Gen. 10:24) By the way, I made up the part about her being 4'11".

A: (c) The wicked man, as graphically described in Job 15:27.

A: (c) 1982. The trick here is in seeing the word *new* as this is a revision of the traditional King James Bible.

Q: The Book of Proverbs says that a meal of
_____ eaten in harmony is better than a
meal of fattened calf eaten in strife.
(a) veggies   (b) grass from the field
(c) fruit   (d) nuts and bushes

Q: Who was the only female judge of Israel?
(a) Judge Judy   (b) Judge Deborah
(c) Judge Martha   (d) Judge Reinhold

Q: See if you can decipher the English name for
these books of the Bible based on their Hebrew
titles.
1). Apocalupsis
2). Pros Philippesious
3). Iakobou (Hint: An epistle)

A: (a) Veggies. (Prov. 5:7)

A: (b) Deborah, found in Judges 4:5.

A: 1). Revelation. 2). The Letter to Philippians. 3). The Letter to James.

Fear not! You are in a profanity free zone, however each of the following questions on the next 2 pages asks for a four-letter biblical answer.

Q: What New Testament book reports the history of early Christians?

Q: What "sea" mentioned in the Bible is actually a salty, landlocked lake?

Q: What apostle preached to the intellectuals of Athens?

Q: What did Noah send out of the ark after the Flood?

Q: John the Baptist referred to Jesus as the _____ of God.

Q: Who was the world's first recorded murderer and who was his victim?

A: _Acts_.

A: The _Dead_ Sea.

A: _Paul_. (Acts 17:16)

A: A single _dove_. Extra credit for the other bird Noah sent from the ark—Raven. (Gen. 8:8)

A: _Lamb_. (John 1:29)

A: _Cain_ killed his brother _Abel_ in Genesis 4.

Q: James had a brother who was also an apostle.
Name him.

Q: How many loaves of bread did Jesus use to feed
the five thousand?

Q: Where Adam and Eve hung out?

Q: Which apostle wrote five books of the New
Testament?

Q: Who wrote the Book of Acts?

Q: What animal's carcass did Samson eat the honey
from a honeycomb out of?

A: *John*. (Matt. 4:21)

A: *Five*—and you can do your own math. (Matt. 14:15)

A: The Garden of *Eden*. (Gen. 2:8)

A: Most guess it was Paul, but it was *John* who penned the Gospel, 1 John, 2 John, 3 John, and Revelation.

A: Many believe incorrectly that Paul wrote Acts; it was *Luke*.

A: Lion. (Judg. 14:8)

Q: Unscramble this famous Bible quotation:
by man not live alone bread shall

Q: In which book of the Bible can the above quote
be found?
(a) Hebrews   (b) Matthew
(c) Luke

Q: According to Hosea, which two vices "take away
the heart"?
(a) smoking and drinking
(b) drinking and gambling
(c) prostitution and drinking

Q: What king (and poet) compared the deceitful
tongue to a sharp razor?
(a) King Remington   (b) King Saul
(c) King Samuel   (d) King David

A: "Man shall not live by bread alone."

A: (b) Matthew 4:4.

A: (c) Hosea referred to them as "whoredom and wine." (Hos. 4:11)

A: (d) David in Psalm 52:2.